THE JEWELLED SHILLELAGH

The Jewelled Shillelagh

An epistle of divine violence

DUNCAN BRUCE HOSE

PUNCHER & WATTMANN

First published in 2019
Published by Puncher and Wattmann
PO Box 279
Waratah NSW 2298

http://www.puncherandwattmann.com
puncherandwattmann@bigpond.com

ISBN: 9781925780475

A catalogue record for this book is available from the National Library Australia.

Cover design by Miranda Douglas
Text design by Christine Bruderlin
Photography by Marie Schuller
Printed by Lightning Source International

This project has been assisted by the Australian Government through the Australia Council, its arts funding and advisory body.

Contents

Animal Prestige.

HELLO FAERE CUNTIES!

Free to you are my pestiferous attentions.
I love this room here where we are I love it . . . here only we are free . . .
No one cares whre eloquence comes from so long as it comes and it
    comes and it comes
Built backwards to ram everthing to death it is our culture I'm sorry.

I ought to take my wages in kisses I know bot
Headbutts are the major bullion
          So come here . . . .

For years Ave told anybody my family were given a fiefdom for loyalty
           In the lowlands of Scotland   by that baldest fiend
                    The Duke of
Normandy (French Pommerania)

Today I find they came from a ditch between Neaufleas Saint Martin
    and Boury-en- Vexin
Miles from Corny, even further from Longchamps, hopelessly remote
    from Perth

Nowdays I walk the streets as a declasse Candy Baron
        Letting the September airs bathe my head
Yir wirth yir weight in hot dried cocky turds   my father sayed
                 being spastically smeart

I am become wild with spite   so wild dense truffles grow there

Howd you get right of way here? On the turnpikey?
How even did you elect to get the best of their manners?
Bescause, my lttle Chippaquiddick,
A'hm a real live dandy or demon pile

Im going back in my mind to Walmajari Country
To finish my apprenticeship
   A shillelagh in one hand
A Kangaroo mallee root in t' other one
                Needs all the clobberers one can
Handle.

Rich in Ballinphunta

Kissed by Banjo
 burbury drunk and satan-haloed
 on the late and wet St George's Road
Just scause I've got a skull, b. bone and tail
Does that mean I'm still Snakey? Each little terrifying scale
Holds its own torrid history of cinema . . . the oily movement of all the
     legendary litte faceys
                    That I have pastimes occulted   growing in a trefoiliate mass
                           Superexploding clover   take me over and over

who is Beau-Dean McDonagh?
where can I find more felt-pressed
angels to amply or simply terrorise the West?

Les Saboteurs   the most tender assbiters of these sixteen counties
& you, you prick, casually emerging from the lair of the golden moley
 Feeding silkily on the moist bellshot of our post-apocalytic haze
 Turning it through your jenny wheel into shimmering garments
 All of our possible weaelth smelted in to a golden stirrup (up! Get Up!)
 Fr. Which there is no Horsie

Lifting the architrove by virtue of the most tender wench (what a
     morning's work!)
An occasion marked by its bonhomie and bonfemie
 I'd like to be salubriated inside and out thankyou

In my dream someone being tortured on a workbench and the village
     children
 All stop you sweety to ask of you the same question:
 Schmutzfinken Zie?

Who is this hornless   wingless tail-less Shulamite
Cradling the jowel of the horsie?
It must be the Angel of Bunrattie!

Duncanpoiesie   (Duncan made me)

Rabattement

'beneath the trash there is some sort of bugle'
Frank O'Hara

Now have I gathered all the Black Chargers of my   Possession
Lk a scaulding from one or some of the Legendary Dykes of the
    Bacchus'Marshes
A good   a lovely   a solid
                           Battering
Lk leaving your child in a ditch of serpents to be properly socialised

Cannot I be at least as ugly as Byron as Brave Sir Robin
                          As Maldoror?
The dopey pastoral is littered with bullys   with Buckeens
                  With Nasty bawbells
Fear naught m. gentle bogey or gentlerougie
If they are s'much more the cunt
Certainly what we see in operation is the Science of Motley

The magpie lark will come to drink from the dint in yr shoulder
Won't you cock me a little coaxy in yr. coaxorium malady?
Something from the Ned Kelly Institute of being opal-eyed &
             Over- whelmingly   smoochable

Bunratty stalking Bunratty
The bull that, heaving, brought up all-its blott
                Tottering   nicely
Am I the last of my caste?   Enjoy
A sort of snakey glittry (glittery) glamour of ascent
    Singing the sang we learnt from Auld Hornie
        Appraising
The Boys with Whom We Burnt the Goat-House Down.

Rathaus Spandau

Emerging from our orgy at the tickleodeon
    A little shabbois (de- shabbie)
Yet have to having enough chopped liver in the fridge to last til' Sundy
    w/ many many placid cornichons
  & a heaving scruff of bread in attendance

Th'petite poke of your belly the prouder rotundae
                 Of your tits   with their cymbalic triumph
   of Turkish bits at the tip
Speak well o'th'morning   of a continuity in juiciness
I mean aside from sex drunkennnness sixty-odd poems and sleep I
    cannot credit
 Thçommotion of this civilization
               What is emotionally blasphemin'
You should go you should go you should keep   going
Retrieve Bucephallus from the very cute valet
  Check his hoof, his heart, his baw-bells, his saddle marks

The nerve which extendeth and extendeth
  Leads the mind to ambleth and ambleth
Passing by the toy shops and knick-knackatories

Did youget in the too much baggie last night?
The baggie let me down again last night. O sprinkle cocaine
o'er the lamentina of this   gentle gambler's century
Ding Boy: a rogue   a hector   a bully
             Or sharper (cant)
To be the compleatest cheat of all of all
The Werewolf of Chatelons   The Demon Tailer
 Nt that far but I do belive in misbehavin & recreational
                           Deviltry.

Traitor's Chantey

Counting the dinglets of my musicking Double Darbies

Being too Bastinadoed for dancing tonight I'll take my intol'able
    pleisure right nere.
Would you rather get plucked off by elsa martinelli
Or watch sian roarty clear a little bit of your warm live shot from her lip?

Chanson de chanson de chanson multiply
My expressions and ebullitions guilty and all such
                Professions
                              Of the witty equivoque
Where is John Wilmot my Lord Rochester?
   Full of prank and sod at the Bunratty Great Hall no
        Doubtles

Arch Dells and Arch Doxes teaze me baby teaze me

                                   Bad.
                          Be a real Biter.

I had meant to pass politely through the underworld on m.way to
                                 See
that spunk
    Eurydice
 Now I note a trinity of cherubs on a fretting sandstone
  Sourced I spose from the same toy shop or knick-knackatory
        All the blighters have the face of me
The grave is mine own.

Bunratty Dishchargre

I spent th'ole of last night Wooing a Lady
By trying to explain How Drag Tyres Work
Tro' a rhythm of collapse, flatulate   excite   stand

                              Brim
                               Fly . . .

Next I'll try the clutch, its intricate tickling disks
It's goading self-completion, its inflamed opposition and functionnant
                                        Antagonisme
In ever'y run the engine supercedes by destroying itself
Sparkplugs   melt   pistons   jibber   the whole goes in for a
      kind of slavish Pagan
                                        Combustion
Ferrying its modest and beplumed chevalier
            To 1 x chequered Hell.

Being in possession and being possessed by 'tis a flange system a sort
      Of ludicrously porous intercourse

Take one songbird drowned in jet fuel
            Nitrous Methane not bas. Armangnac
            You've Force fed it in the dark for months
When eating, burst its heart last with the tongue at the top of the palate

Every 392 Hemi dreams of being an Ed Pink Racing Engine
Set by the Chef to consume itself
                        a terrible delicacy

Bunratty Stalking Bunratty

Born in Balleymaloney by now I've had my revenge on everybody
                                        sentimentally speaking
my verminarious friends and the others
  To wake with the tongue as flammen-throwen
An oily and live peccing of the impeccables
            Even as the antique sun loves its own reckless incontinence
 It is my fancy I do declaire

Dear Addy   Do you remember ourselves at the Siege of Bunratty? It
      was ever
                                        My favourite sacking

Headed to the Dervon or Van Diemen's Land for the Solisitice
w/ ma   caterwauling digestion
  to slap that bitcheen Percy Beauchamp & then make up again
    completely
Daen the bull dance with the dancing bull
                          It is my fancy I do de Claire
    Immobilius in mobilium
 Alive with the spermies   diving down down down
Ir legendary harmonium forged in the shipyards of Limerick City

                          & I propose to have perplexed my affairs
The silver knife rocks on the table to the rhythm of your ratteyed nerve
Courage   my little Battleship Potemkins, we still have the hellover
    way to go though this
        right now
                    seem hellischly pleasant

9

Queenie.   (Abbotsford VII)

Time to set down the Blackbird drill & Blackbird
                                                    Hammer
It is the hour of the veined trumpet and blo'wn surplice   yes
        The Ern Malley Hour
Everwhere citizens practice felatio holding it there with the softest O
 Th'inside lip can manage, else it's cunnilingus, rich
   Victuals
In the Sacking of the Golden Pubis.
                            I can just make out the sign of the Cock O'Lappin

Souviens-tu   Living under the Bat-track   the black
                            Organizational horde who fly by desire
                                        From the kings Domain to
        the cool grottoes
                                                    Of the convent
@ the Carrionblush Hotel   Sister Palace
To the Cock a'Lairpin   w'its secret savage gymnasiums
Trains here travel tro' d'air and arrive us at the Underworld.

The hands what built this embankment are from
                            Morpeth
Corcaigh City, Slough, Ballylickey, Ballyranald
                        Armagh   Tyrone
                    Rottnest
Londinium probably.
Dentures   single pearls of work   surfacing
                                        From the dead
                    Thr. Tongues are harder to swallow

Where are you Pony? Farmer Peart.

Take me to the Laird O'Cockpen
                    Or Carrionblush Hotel I think
          I'm feeling a little fancy.

Bodyke County

The O'Halloran Sisters of Bodyke County
                    pour hot mizzle
 Oér the raging bailiffs
That's almost all we need to know
Fidgety at the wheel of la grand poubelle

Fetch my peruke!

E went out a last naught and got hammered with the Christians agaiane
        O Lordy
Scots Irish Cornish and the Bitches of Bunratty Great Hall
I'm looking for a permanent laement I mean
    Something must be burnt
        It's   libational!
 With a horny with a mostly Satanic intent. (Hello Nevie)

Cream of logistics Cream
                    of the Laird of Crowthorn
Come back mouldy aristocracy we didn't mean it I don'think
        Melbourne warlords of the future ramparts of the rich
        Allow me to be your chanteyman
                                Counterfeiter of tiptricks
As the prophetess call me Madame Chauncey

Your little fang-teeth seems as delicate as my susceptibles I fancy
        m.daerling
We shold be together committed to harlotry***

***   See also The Sheela-na-Gig conundrum.

Bunrattty Joust

Dear Claire Stinkboot
                    All Rabbits are   flash
                                    Yes
But what's Bocastle?
        It's the dope   the dopey gap in your teeth   Freckleodeon
All pale and rooted   as you aire as you aire
                            Dutiful marplot of the pissheads of Penzance
    Let's do it while the hellover is fresh

We continue to sing
sing like the spoiling satisfaction of the bowel longe after the bacchanal
        has ended
At Castle Bunratty there is always a room on fire somewhere
                                            Mostly to goad the cockles

Mixa:mitosis ought to mean thinking and making in a ragedy fashion
                    Thinking in rags
I'll teach you a dance clld 'scalding the bailifs'
    taught to moi by O'halloran sisters of the Bodyke county
    Honoraria Annie and Sarah

    Paddy Hartnett sobers (hardly) on the scorched ground   w/ a tin cup
        over his ear for shelter
    In the ultraviolet highlands
                    Of that place called Van diemans Land
        The name portending a superior smirch

We continue to sing   sing like the spoiling satisfaction of the bowel
     longe after the bacchanal
has ended
     Demon Flyer you dry your black and white silks down the sexy
     quarter mile

               Your mouth squar'd as the insatiable intake of a Ramcharger
               Which sqozes the air so mostly into your meat baubels

     Behind the lance and visor there is, once again, 'nobody.'
Would you rather the Clonakilty Blood Sausage Prize for being yurself
Or the International Bull's Pizzle Prize
                         For Pinked Excitement . . . protrusive   even
                    prosthetic
Raggedy as an army of parasitized Aphids
     Your anxieties   you need them   they are your engine.

Old Ram of Dalgety

Rippishly inspissated..
How would you like to be tied outside a pub for forty years !!!!!!!!!!!!
    (j'espere)
Cloven hold in the settled turf amidst
            the adulterate confetti

Would you rather appear to your public as the Rarling Cove or a Rum
    Duke
 Covered in Auxillary Beauty
   Licking the lippes with red setting the eyebrows
     Riding one's malformations with style
Ave got eighty feet of liquid gold braid in the pantry

Release me but let me back in occasionally to Club Vanity
Where one can Administer and receive *le grand coup*
 The claque of enlightenment & possibly win
a can of boutique bugspray to Mollify and
mortify
   yr neighbours
   More dainty a method than Crucifixion
You wanton Mutwigg.

Trying to find the messworks up in Tilba Tilba (go straight past Central
    Tilba)
                        Something witchetyprobed for goodness
                            Right out in Dibirdibi Country
once yir a grot and you know yir a grot you
become more of a grot
clots and clots and clots of grot
                    pardon!

Th'butchers wife the butchers daughter the butchers hams the butchers
        fatty glamour
superintuitive become superinsensitive
an each-way bet on the dueling chainsaw dandies
maturing speed of psychosis as we head
            forever Westwards.

Demolition Derby Shantey

The sparkplugs having all become glowplugs
We live in the cast-iron globe of perpetual
 irritant ignition & I

I am back in Bitchy-Town

Travelling with you is like travelling with a child, a child who can drive
    and smoke
                        Which I vastly appreciate
Let's not talk of coded intimacies unless we talk of the Civil War
We're not just fighting for the condition of keeping slaves
                                        but for the shapes of our

    swagger as we do
                                                        So

    In the god-drunk airs of Sweet Cobargo

Our ebullious expreffions and confessions most of all
What will it belike to re-enter the dingbat atmosphere
                        Of a détente

Both of us picking up our teeth and the aftermath of working out
    which are whose
A kind of embloocied folkdance up to and including the limits
                                        Of riddicculousness

O jaysus Fleckert Dandycorn Christ
            It is getting dark

I did like violent rhetoric of the peaceloving anarchists
(the champs de Mars's a remnant orchard)
    radical democracy, Jacobinism, populism, atheism
 there's still not enough blood abroad to float a republic of the heart
I think my guts have had enough

Though I have on my desk the death-mask of my nemesis entitled
                                        'Golden Steak'
Our fervid bio-squalor burned down to n egg-cup's worth of snuff

 Did you note in the intermission that we had become completely
    Bourbonized?
Solve et Coagula   we are the living ringer of the Baphometti
Arch Dells and Arch Doxes . . .   teaze me baby
                  teaze me bad

                                    Be a real biter.

Busterbrain's Daytrip Blues

Happy is the illicit.
The charm of Byron's doggerel
The purloined cowboy buckle, the birthday kiss
That is offered in chastity but performed erotically.

I eat ma
 Snake Kilpatrick
 In the flagship restaurant of the Savoy Hotel
  & Listen to
Vladimir Putin's patois his
          Sublime accents we
   Got here from Minsk
                 Via a
V8 snowmobile I
       Think he's saying
'I take your pleasure seriously'
He's so unlike me
Little bit bitter
   That'll be the morphine patches
Ghost of Merle
             Haggard
   In the engine

Riding Pillion it's not very
            Macho I' admit
 or perhaps it is
I loved having m' arms around his middle
         My very own Putin
           Mon precieux
      My Butcher of Chechnya

19

Only a tiny bit of muck
                On the seat
For my dowry I offer fifty
    Jars of Dalgety preserve
& instructions to the séance machine
-let's get on the phone to some poltergeisten . . .
Like all the great Popes
                    Bonny
        I am self-ordained
Even in fant'sy
Things have to end we had to part
'Fuck you lttle Rabbit!'
 Au Revoir Blizzard-tits

True bit sexy lightning carries on out to sea

Candelo Speedway

Going bitch-kegs at it
After our Demon Tweak
Seven thousand pistonlicks per second

B.now I have stolen my own weight in pork products
Reader, self-annihilating and semi-devine! Do this in memorium of me.
As revenge against the ones who gave us a taste for infinite things

All our love of Australian Aeronautics
  Is concentrated in the corvid   crow   corby
A kind of songfoul and airborne Satanic Pastie

Half Cornish Half Irish me ma
Has a taste for Scotch Greys
In the Celtic League it maketh me
        A treble cleff'd bastard
Familiar t'all   loyal
              To not
                One.

Fornication   aplenty
Of Lies?   A great cov'rage
Barbarism   we try and we try

Unlike Juptire we want to effect a more delicate lechery
Appearing to Leda as neither Bull nor Swan but as a declasse Candy
    Baron
Having a vivid little roister behind the kirk at Bellbrae

To make mushrooms burst on the side of the blood oven
An organical democracy where every cell might think for itself

And is at war with every other.

In this messy era of the rule of the South Gundagai Molls.
Giddy up.

The Jewelled Shillelagh

If my chimes are called Dougal Beattys then your moistened charm is a
     Belpaire Firebox.
Now how can I commit to a dark tirade
 W/ out the pendulistic wit of my jeweled Shillayley?

Punked Cherrys of the Squirearchy
Note my Queen of the Plains Disposition!

'ee's got this wild bloody . . .
   ee's got a debbil _n 'im!'

There's more than a *bit* of cock-a-doodle-doo on the air this morning
                                        m. grievous
     Beatriz (trobairitz)

you've got the burnt bulbs *meine grosse poopinschpott* but darkly lovely
you will always worry   but knowest thou this?

   Gabrielle 'bonneur' Coco Chanel waits for you in secular heaven
   Seated in faberge spittoon   with an infinite
                                        jar of *truffle au victoire*
           for to grease your Dougald f.ckin Beattys

Save me a seat Butch
Save me a litre of your most Christian champagne.
Now should I look for and find a shittyie job or stay at home and read
     Dostoievskii's
 Patient Destruktion of our regular revolutionary potential
          titled   'Demons'

Death's tiny wig the brightest thing in this room

Fizza Tron Ferguson enters the sea at Bellambi 1974
  She's not a woman any more
        She became a bean-sí
A sort of socially committed imp
            like Circe or Saint Dolly Partone

I will get my armour hammered out
making uncreased these sundry wounds and curses
                  my gallons hang fairly
  my guts are ever in their favourite place
fit with the repaste of stolen foodstuffs and vainglorious wines

You won't see another gathering of the Peach Fuzz Union of Australia
      any time soon
                        By which I mean a collective of luscious
                              balding demons like me
                                    *
                It's an old trik
    to mention the Serpent
    to suddenly see the schismatic cells of borrowed light
Fangs up a poem and gets it moving   In service of Señor Snakeh
      Perfect effort of counterfeasance

you are my jeweeled shillelagh

THE SHANTY ON THE HILL

The Unicorn is a symbol of lust, is it?

Languishing at the top of Rooty-toot Hill
           Recently stroaked
              By lightning
Ave got a tied bunch of whorethumb and spitmidget
  In m. gentleman's top-pocket a token
     Of insolent that is adolescent beauty

Ave worked all week at the Tathra yardsales and m.packet is full of
    quiddities
            Show me what's left of the pig on the spit
              From which all have eated and taken
                  Thr superannuity
  A cultural technicue banned in both Testaments

Black working milk trucks of high polish
Enter Errol's honkeytonk dream
Caravans with names like 'excaliber' 'nobleman' 'crusader' 'Hero of
    Dunkirk'
'Pamplona' (hene)   'Unicorn' (Ooooh . . .)
                         Go by the natural highway
A game in which just naming things exposes their 'right' melancholia
O Cobargy bargo laid out under the Snowys

I dress in Madame Palomas's knickers
  Polish blue with lacey trim
& a pinaforte studded with cherries that says 'eat me'
It's not kinky or New York
More calm and satiable

Which suits the steamy terraforming madness of Autumn in these parts
Ill sit in the canary-room and produce a long handwritten letter
 To Leah 'grace in shady tennis' Muddle
  The last declasse heiress of Carlton

Shae is the anti-chauvaniste

Remember that documentary we saw on AC/DC
  Feat. Reg 'Bonald' Scott
Ballantyne soaked troubadour from Scottish Perth
                                        (Freo) drinks champagne
      from a turkey carcass
                              & has his own Percy
He was full as I suppose of that most subtle bacteria: the ones that
      chatter t'each other
Compelling him as the third party to overcome the dirtiness and
      drudgeryness
                              O'th'world
                              With Ryewhiskey

Champig!

A Champagne drinking pig
I met at a 'Skills for the Apocalypse' party

We would come to your
  Wedding chérie bot
  The Liddle Leprachauns have got
              no money

ir intellectual bourgeoisie rent belonging and write 'country'
I'd rather walk
  Mogil Mogil
    To
Lightning Ridge
Fed along the Milkje Way (the pointer stars are cockatoo (Gogadoo))
    Gundabloui Road drops in and out of 'heaven'
(Collymongle Rugby Bikini Pagan Creek Poison Gate
    Merrywinebone Bulyeroi Old Burren
                                        Pokataroo)
To pick up an icy longneck for some actually calibrated
                              Oblivion
Composing this demon bagatelle

Melbbourne affectionately dubbed 'Cloaca Maximus'
m.feet stewing as feasty convict pies in these sensible shoes
The Singular Beastie is coming coming my dear did you think we
    were not
            Joking?

Dalgety Dalgety

There's the Bunny
Flashin his Bunny.

Yr seriousness has spread over the parlour
    Like a goddam Cumulonimbus Incus
I stare at your broken heroes Nose
                & Finger my soft Shillelagh

I am as Historically Fond of you as a pissup at a shipwreck
Or a brief détente between two unquenchable foes
What we want is an explanation not of charisma but of shipwreck
    whiskey
 Which swells with charisma
   Become the excruciable arbiter   in a fancy dram
     Of dead to dying souls

Connoisseurship of the destruction of everything to make way
                            For Muttoncraft
On the High Monaro Plains
 The desecration of the Snowy   Country and its lovelies full of
    heroin picks and holes
Dalgety Dalgety
I think I want to walk to the bottom of Lake Jindabyne and live in the
    drowned town there
 Make out with passing drovers
 Thr little pussies biting thr bicycle seats

Quite out

Of my mind on Trucker Speed our adrenal gland seems to have taken
    its own

                                                    Captain's Ticket

Playing the throttle O
                    Tempertation!
  Drop me off at Rosie Wroe's
Night riven with some bucolic brawl over the Cobargie Bridge
& the sweet-time ditty of a small-block Chevy
    S'it rides up and down the sacred mountain

In the exchangeable fluids of lovers comes
 The melee of family demons
Let's leave on each other a fresh Gorgoneion
 A Dalgety bruise (masterpiece!)
  A Dalgety lovebite

Hot in the Priory

TOTAL DARLINGS
I would kill for our confederacy of love perhaps
          I shouldn't kill you

What is hot in the priory.
  Some dapper Moqueur   takes up the lightning tip
        To do its casual mocking, to fattern (flatter) so slightly in song
M'lush paranoia
Peart of our pleasure in roiling the country is to become a bit more
    camembert,
    Roquefort, Ranelagh Randyman
        A gothic revival not of but in the trouser-packet

  Mesdames et mes'sieurs Im sure
  you can spare me an evil look you
Are one of the few people who'se displeasure gives me no pleasure

I understand the temptation to read parakeets of the super-earthly blue
    as *purity*
Rather than *Perceval Perceval!*
               I mean birds has
             Insides too don't they?
        & Mollie Dogs & Capuchins

There is a dark glimmering inside if you seek it (thanks, Frank)
  Your talent not the gift of light but a Pocket of dirty matches
\signed
      Senor Snakeh.

Duelo a Cudgelo   (Duel with Cudgels)

Whether its returning from Black Mass @ The Friend in Hand Hotel
                                            (mmm . . .   peaty)
 Or from killing a troll on the mountain
               I want you to properly meet my jeweled shillelagh.

Whether it's a cudgel against indifference or the cudgel of indifference
    ill never know.
Hello Steeplechasers
   we've been it seems so long at the Burlycue
               <applause>

               Fuck Saint-Beuve!

Good Friday in Fitzroy and feeling so
      Gabrielle 'bonheur' Coco Chanel
Coco was a junkie   a distillated poppy-fiend a lover
                    of Polish Mischa's
                           'Lethal wit.'

I mean haven't they just awarded you
    The Transvaal Diamond Chewer's Medal
                 For best-booted Harpie?
           m. ittle Derryscallop. . . m. testy shrewlewd . . .
You donkey your own jugs! From now on

If you see me approaching you in an Eastrn and Northrn Gippsland
      Axeman's Association singlet covered in Jizz
        Accomplished in war Diminished in Love
          Will not mean a more spotted afffection
            Merely a coming dotage court'sy of my jeweled shillayley

Classically cloacaphonic
There's no guarantee yull be remembered forever unless yur a sappho
  or catullus
        Or a caphullo or syphullus or any other of the
    innumerable forgettables

I beat you with my shillelagh

Bad Daemon

Begatten   Begettin   Begotten
Shady
  Feinagler

The reviews are out on the morning airs
                              Hypokrite of your
Performance the evening before, when the charmed mist
Set to flame the earth's old wounds.

Some compared you to Paris, flaunting it before
  The testosteroidal din of the Greek army
Others to M.Dietrich, eating all at once her pink roses in a room at the
    Savoy Hotel
While the best saw two crumbed lamb-chops, a tiny boater of
                              Gravy

& a fast-eyed pregnant bitch waiting for the bones

Maundyists!
Follow the trails of cowpye and chooksong
Away from the Town of Ironmungy
Past DULCEYS PIGGERY
(hello Shurly, Digoy, Patsy, Dixie, Bonnie, Brandy)

Back to the citadel of the Blonde Cockroach-we want to exceed
In feats of arms and in feats of love
  Move between the lace doilyists
    & the classically spastiche Avant-garde
Our way will be lit by the wistful flickering
                              Of a bad daemon.

Dougal Beatty 'plague of versecraft'
  Is back playing the mumblebone.
Dressed in the fleece of the mumblebone stud.

Shrunken Head Shanty

The first gem I scarped from my Viking Dictionary was 'Byrdefuld'
Burden . . . what Burdensome.
See those four women over there? If I were to start a collection of
    shrunken heads
Those are the rare portions ye want.

A'm off the Beetlejuice 'til Thursday so
Fetch me my Peruke.
Is it too early to mention the Peruke?
The charmed human knacks
        &   Knuckles keep rolling one by one off the dash
As you negotiate the bends & warped bridges
                of Bodyke County
What would Francois Villon do?

I feel I have his shrunken head in my shrunken head
w/ma hands in the slits of the poacher's raddle-bag
m.thumb in the sticky purse of his corn hole pipe
        what am I saying?

Celtic heroes approach in their little blue copper boats
    Pushed by the storm they pity us our paganlessness & Weep
                Whiskey
Tongues out my little derby-brides my
clean-gutted cupid-ties
watch what it does to the lush pitch and pornographic hue
 of the turf   feel
    the soft finger-pugs of Molly Paloma
the froggie that loveth the snakey
                Oh

What darkens our humours is the cinder from the stacks of the
    Dreadnought *Dalgety*
We'll wreck her

My brain become a figment of jade
WHERES MA BETELGUESE
A'm ever sae fond of it likely

TOM O'HEARNS DRAUGHT

'*babylons not a place*'   Nick Whittock

The Hag's Purse   Cock o'Gobble
The demon fiddler twisty in the   Pines
   The magic jawbone rings

Billy Boy Bayley!
        All empires feel like this at the
                        end.
Fir the two fellas who wrecked the Corkman Hotel I want you to take
                    This song as your curse. take it.
Feelin so bolshie which means being
            Like an uppity peasant as felt
            By the Bourgoisie
   Like the fat fuckin farmer who talks tender
                To his workhorse
                    O'er the phone (Yr. a *darling*)

I may take a retreat to Tasmania
                tht mythical bitch
to whair m. old folks bones are
   not th' old old propser folks
   but the only ones I know
                so tell me

It's weird working with Dahlia
    The only employer now is the demolition derby 'tseems
It's even weirder putting toto crème on the
                Death-Knobs
        w/ a renovated savagery!

That would be the end for that story

Libertine Arts Scholarship

I can think of no better waste of time than to go on a poet's tour
    of Dalgety
Taking in the killing floor and dark offal pots
 Of the Nimmatabel Meatworks
 W/its headless handless and tail-less kangaroo hugging a teddy

Checking in on the improbably long expert Dong
                Never Forget!
 Of the high plains Donkey at Jincumbilly
 Lona in her sarong watching daytime teevee
Humming the melody of a toilet-brush shantey

While the shearers sing their songs of breaking down the cheque
            On baggies of crystal meth

Can you imagine the mayor of your town
 Gadding around in the flayed hide of their natural enemy for
    twenty days
All for the glory of Huitzilopochtli (pronounce *Weetzeelopoachtli*)
 Ripping the still beating heart out of a dole-bludger?

The Tathra Wildcat that
 Independent understudy of the Wolf of Rimini
Is s.much more himself with a young rabbit a dangling
 From his mouth he has   Bloody
                Heccaeity
What about you my misbegotten gnode of sincerity
        My fabled dribbler?

Therere notes stuck all over the engineer's operating panel

38

Of the Dreadnought *Dalgety*
From Shez (Sheryl) The White Witch of the Caravan Park
With subtle instructions of how to proceed
  With Telepathic Devilry

My old white horse has floating bones
  & Must get me to a funeral soon
  But fuckit let's go on a gallop to Dalgety
    So late in the psychedelic season.

Rat-Tasting Bandicoot

Attention Citizens of Ironmungey!
The tongue is the most subtle of the muscles
But it dinne work without the plush and dome
  & teethy mob of its parliament

-GET THE GOLD-   I tell my disciples
Open up the ancient blue jets of rhetoric
 Burn me while you persuade me
                    The intimacy of the inquisitori
                          Or any torture really
Happy immolation and I become my own crackling
Like a art movie or a spy movie with lots of P.J Harvey
                    Fckn great go p.j west country lady

Remember ir irish summer we flew over the underwater dunes
Or jellyfished it really
                  The strand at dingle
The razor-backed blaskets failing at signaling 'cruel nature'

We moved in the water with the animal sleekness of individual sperm
        High on Seamus's mushrooms
           Maeve has crawled up into the sea-cave
            Singing like an egg in the Sheela-na-gig.

Pugnator Pugnacious

I.

It's Dirty-Bird Hose calling from downtown
   Cobargie
The sun punches through the tartan scrabble
& comes to shave the marble cheek of the conquerer's horsie
     To comfort the equestrian statue in the Visigoth and Tartar
                                 Memorial Park.

I bought pigs at the right intervals and worshipp'd the neon Playboy
                             Bunny
                     Dress'd some time to pass as working class
But if I believe in Patron Saintronage
It would have to be grey-eyed Shea Wyatt
Partly Because of the dream I 'had' of her ma lying across my lap
      Smoking on the bench seat of a compact Chevrolet

Wait a moment would you while I put a ladle
 Of this fabulous stuff on m.dinner

If yir going to reinstate feudal
   Systems of relation then I'll
 Be the fckn pixie   poacher
Burning all the public timber of the Brogo
      Bega and Mogo valleys all the way to Brindabella

For my domestic combustion chamber & a quiet night in with
   Supercandourous
                  Betelgeuse
'There' where Deus is a fat catastrophe
     And not a Dialectic (whoops)

More bloody heccaeity
Render that hog fat bebe til the tears run

                              Clear'n the Sorrow's
                                    Genuine.

II

I have turned my forces to courtly love and have chosen Betelgeuse as
      my paramour.
Betelguese I can feel your limb darkener coming all around me
                                    I can feel it.
God if you want purity is what you want
                  Betelgeux
Stars whose names betray their erotic function . . .

                                                Betelguise

            Late night walks with only Beetlejuice
            Cyber-masturbation watched only by Betelgeuse
              You may make fun of my vice but you do not know
The dirty elixir of being loved by Btelgeuse

You warm yourself manually in the less subtle
                  Radiomotion of the sun
Forgetting Pollux Polaris   Bellatrix   and the favourite who is the
      head of a God
                  Betelgeuse

You know that by his cheek it is all raucousness
 Yet from here he is as quiet as Lombardy in plague-time
Whr the grapes fall to earth and the goats get
drunky drunk

Not the plague as it appeared at the Rocks in Sydney
Which seemed to suffer from allsorts of official interference
The Rum Corps having devolved to bureauocratic banditry
                   & righteous smacking of the black rat

Check this Red-bearded campaign of seduction
If you must be a wage-punk do it for yerself
Selling hogbutter and porkshandy out the window of a small caravan
@ the Wolumla markets
   'tis a rounded humiliation but I do it
      For Betelgeuse

It is I suppose as simple as falling out of the natural order
We shall never again hear the stones speak or know
                         totemic botheration
So I am sending my love darts and am open to receive them
 To a late stage redhead supernova
   belching light years
Who produces bubbles of gas I've heard as big as himself
   That cosmic bitch Betelgeuse

'god loveyer marguerite, we're over the worst of it!'
Sound of precocious fuse
       Spitting

III
You have the look of the Wolf of Rimini hearing
  In a unique ceremony, he had been canonized into hell as
When the fire falls into itself to burn more
                  Repletely

Golden Bogey

I am insuperably lazy and this makes me proud.
Midnight in Derby
a new suburb of Melbourne
        Where Fitzleroy used to be
The Bacchae pass by
    my window with their paraphernaliac
cocks I wonder

    O Succoy Bacchantes, incubus and succubi
    Whom
        Shall we be tearing apart
Tonight?
    Because what elas is there to do?

Anyone can snap the branch of an apple tree I want
    To put my juicy tattoo on the breast of the dizzy pulque plant
                The mother goddess hirselfe
    To tease the wrath of the Gorgone
Whose sap is not flammable but explosive
Whose forgiveness is stinging

Commissioned graffitti never as good as the rough stuff
                        We like the rough stuff
Sacrificial jingo of the golden bogey
The R(oyal) B(otanical) G(ardens) a giant phantasmagoria of chlorophyll
Blended by a couple of European extremists
A paradise authorized by Count Ferdinand von Mueller
    Then updated in taste by William Guile-e-foyle

The satyric art deco garden Melbourne deserves though I must confess
 I too have used it as an apparatus of seduction

All the plants have had their teeth removed
The awesome maw of the vegetative gut sewn shut
Gazetted Nupitals   and loungey rites of Fertility
                the radical absence of stone idols
 (No golden bogeys)

Contrapuntally placed apart from the rat laneways
Of Russian Collingkvood, Chelsean Fitzroy and
 Carlton/ Edinburgh
You see it is designed to make a little monarch
            Out of every Victorian with a threepenny piece
                A baloney sandwhich and a wormless
                    apple

Marylebone's Wedding (Saturday May 27, Royal Botanical Gardens, Melbourne)

Pagans I don't know what they do with them
Chuck em in the river I Spose
You try drawing the head of Xipe Totec he will take
All your drankeeness, guile and something else which you will not
                                        Be getting back.

Cornkingdom! Feed us your husks . . .
I'm talking spectacles of excess like the Demolition Derby
Not for theory but for my little party at which
                                        I'm sure you'll come
withall the indignity of a collapsed bouffant
 Or the pissed bride and groom sliding down the embankment
                        toward their departing pirogue

I wander as I must the botanical gardens as I must
 It seems to us a colonial fetischery
 Redeemable as a pharmacy- here
 Are the juices of the sacred Maguey Plant
   Succor to the schoolchildren who carve in its flesh
                Details of their crushes

Where are those vegetative triffid gods the poppies
 Who give us little opiate blumens in the blood
   Where the delicious loblolly
Or those higglady pigglady plants that give us peach bonbons
   The fabulous dollar note the terrible marshmallow

Where is their secret armoury
 Their cabinets of technical biofilth?
There must be some campaign to keep the animals away

The aphid the sexy leech of heat the sacred maguey worm

Sort of an obscene reserve for plant-o-philes
I must follow its honkeytonk logic and make it familial to myself
Look, there's a nice bit of Rodneybeard, a savvy but flakey Shirleybush
The Erniegrass is everyone's favourite while the Bessiegrass is often
    intractabley brittle
The Sharynfern is very pretty, poisonous in youth and dying as soon as
    it reaches maturity
                                Having a certain charm of insolence
The Patricia Gum an obvious Matriarch even as a sapling
Kaye Doug Brucie Ken Marg Pat Gus Leigh Brett Shirl Wayne
 They all turned into gang-gangs and pissed off
        Back to Ulverstone

The magpies rouse in the supernaturally heated air
  There is a strange Murphyness to it
The intricate folly I mean

You know they straightened the elbow of the river to build it
       This anti-kink an original blasphemy

Shazzabell

Is that my mother's death-rattle coming through the Radio?
　　Not the Radio Radio
　　　T'other one . . .

It is from my father I get my genetically tight buns　　(ooh . . .　a bit of
　　the braggadaccio!)
　Why not since when did knee-high sock length Scottish peasants get
　　to claim anything
　　　　　　　　　　　　　　Other that a few stones from the beach
　　　　　　　　　　　　　　　　On the Isle of Fleaday
　　　　　　　　　　　　　　　　　Raw and gawky

Though I've come down to the mall I'm calm beaucause
　I've got the Medusa's head in a bag here
　Indomitability!
　Without cheating or not too much anyway

The One the Marsupial Lizard Lady who bequoth me
　　　　　　　　　　　　　　Ma vanity &
m.taste for being molested by the squirrilous airs
And what's the message? That wae've never been
on such a trip as this de-escalator called Morphine　　　　It's exciting
　　　　　　　　　　　　Don't tell　It's lovely

We could be like Remus & Romulus you and I if the Bitch
　　　　　　　　　　　　　Were a Thylacine

What purrs
　Like the Luciferric blaze seen at speed through the trees
Or m.brains . . .　　dashed! on Brunswick Heads　　　go out to meet

The sea

Such was our insc_ency.

Clam Shantey

Clams! . . .

        Clams

These last One Hundred Ten years I have not been at sea

 Have seen clams do some . . . . . . things

Eaten abalone eaten each other
Just look at the fishermen's faces

                       they know

              Clams . . .

        Clams

Fat Cherub Blues

Death by Cherub.
The Go-Betweens
   Triffids   Radio
       Birdman
Australian Cantoists reply to me
  The office of priest is extinct!

Lead me through the intrixcacies of the Italian Renaissance
    (Quattrocento)
M.hair is on fire and I'm tooting my horn at your front gate
         Evil!
This is a sonic riddle for the human voix
There is a great poverty at the heart of infinite choix.

I'm goin on a Alzheimer's Tour of Tasmania
To stick a Scotch Finger Biscuit
 In Shirley's mouth at Derby
 Another in Sharyn's to the south

All our levels are good 'spite (smite)
  The many miles (smote)
   Got a Speedmongers supply of Carrolton United
    Nerve Coolant for we are the Dukes!
  Not of Hazzard but Candelo Marshmallow
          County

Takeaway pack of Snake Kilpatrick
         Pickled ginger slices
& for our mirror-charm the relic of Lona's broken coccyx!

Ooooh . . .   . . . it's the Fauves
I hear the butcher's daughter say
From her backyard dunny seat of the authors
 of this sunset: paynes grey, Mars Black and Blauviolett Hell
Claudio Monteverdi   watch over
    my wingless descent.

A Fine Bogey Tale

The five kings of Ireland gathered together one day to elect one great
    king of Erin to save them from
        Themselves
They chose Dougal Beatty, child and heir of Ripley Bogle
  Born on the waters of the moyley: the body between Erin and Alba

The new slang for being a bum is 'Scottish Bushranger'
 Howe, Brady, Hall, M.D Morgan and even Nedward Kelly
  All believed in sprites leprechauns unaechauns caprichauns
       & tatty-bogles did this help them in their
            Profession?

Between the CockOLairpin and Carrionblush Hotels
Youll find the Yorkshire Stingoes
  With the coldest front door in history I hardly know
  What I'm doing with my life it seems as ungovernable
As I would like to be

No one dies more beautifully as Dido than Sarah Connolly on the Radio
I listen not just in drag but as a perfect replica of Margaret Thatcher
                Those pearls
Th'air whistling between my teeth as she climaxes
         I arch into the sofa
        Schitterende!

  Fricka   Frigg   Freya
        Tragedy is our basic fare

When will I hear a Tough Faggot Shantey
D'you remember when we heard the ghosts of the girls voices

Coming out of the stone of the fireplace on Skye
T'made our pig bristles stand in a kind of virile spook manoeuvre
Wird celtic shit

Would all the descendents of Shadrack Dainty please step forward
Living and Dead

Shld we introdeuce the war-pig to the war-petrol?
Let fly my discandying bandits
Let fly
Unlike other humans I wouldn't mind
Being transformed into a demon of the air

7/07/2017

Cunty Tipperary

M. fresh
From burying
 A Scotch King
  He named his g.daughter
         The next King!
'Twere fckn great

I threw m. green tooth into th'ocean
Now would you get it back for me

God blaw and save from
        Bogles
All these silky cretins I mean your children

His native place was Killenaule this is
        Hell he thought!
I'm blythe to see you.

BITE YOUR GATE

Dextrous in the arts of Miscellaneous spunkcraft
You return to us mincingly
  Your red fur shorn short
What choice do I have but to make this song of fleischeslust

The line of neck to shoulder, from the lobe to the shoulders nub
Is Paris gone to Bateman's Bay
 Same as the walk from Van Diemen's Land to Charlotte's Pass
Both favoured scenes of the travelling ancestral beings who live in
                                    Epic Chantey

Travel lust Kitchen lust Front room curtain-movement lust
              Pepper lust
Peroneal Phenomenon (Lust's sign)   Spankenlust   Lust-
                                              Phanomen
You have freckles on your tits the way Australian Cinema used to could
The blessd furze of your pubis tapers immaculate
The air the morning seems to be unmade by the aural dynamos of the
    alpenloons
  I think they call them Kurrajongs.

It is the season of Xipe Totec (Sheep-he To.tek) Our Lord the Flayed
    One
          Alive to the tiniest thing by being ritually turned inside out
          In all dead forms the impersonator of life
          Not here but in Mexica though we feel it

Broken bottle of Dalgety
          White Horse Whiskey
          Midnight white pikie van be our home

Shreds e tartan be our curtains   bladder
                                                                    Explode
Was going to ask you to listen while I talk of my mother's madness
  But you tell me yours while I cup your ming
                                                        dynasty gland
Why does it get so fckn itchey and why cant I or anyone else do
    anything about it

This is one passage of seduction I don't wish to see completed
 I shall wait at the bottom of your driveaway at the Old Butter Factory
Patient as the rat-eating bandicoot full of prescription diet pills
                    Yet with perfect nerve

It's like waiting for a cyclone (Biddy) that only I can see
Biting your gate

Ballyfanatic

Bliss is shit.
All along the coast Australian colossal towns.
All the fucking scholars in this Possumshoot   -voices-
Th'coo coo! Of dozing pidgeonmeat

Darlington thy
 Gorgeous slumpalaces
    Too easily chearmed he has
More tartans than the titans of bogroll
Scoatish to the point of riddiccule
M.French is shit but I'm going on a good tilt/
    Of the braggart

Shane Macgowan sings weare bound for botany bay through the ghost
    of his real teeth
There is no IRA exservicemen's clubs in sydderney and the jacobites
        haveall gone in for the rag trade
Ill see you in chupachup heaven bebe i.e. the arrondisements of hell
                        Chip'n'dale   Lil' Eppington   Waterloo
All the pretty trolls tournout (a tourney!)   fi' th' wedding of Whom?
 Which Drag King and Queen of our comprador bourgeoisie?

G'bless the nocturnal cabdrivers of New South Wales
Th'old Albanian fella who no longer believes in sex
Th'old Chinese fella whose father died two week ago and whose kids've
    split from the cult of family

I get married to every clam'ring generation of flame that licks up the
    convict chimney

So many of them   hot phantasmagoria of ancestors mine and
     everyone else's
In these seconds read the deshabillage   the strip-tease of matter
Aside from the milch-cow and goat A've got the two pet crows Angie
     Nag and Linda Baguette.

I got a Cowboy Crush on the Air Force Officer
                    Shopping for antiques shae
Looks like Louise Brooks in High Cinched Navy Slacks
                    & medals
My pineals my eyeballs are busting fat!!!
Cue Armed Forces Fairies and Harps where shall I find

Lily looks like
the angel that
'gives it'
to

Saint Thérèse

in Bernini's

Delias

Rod of Gold
I wish I had
sandwhiches
road trip
sandwhiches!
but when I
it was Great.
thanks to
and powerful

little point
of flame
one of Lily's
we went on a
Lily said `I bought
I said 'uh..'
had the sandwhich
Anyway,
our gorgeous
patrons

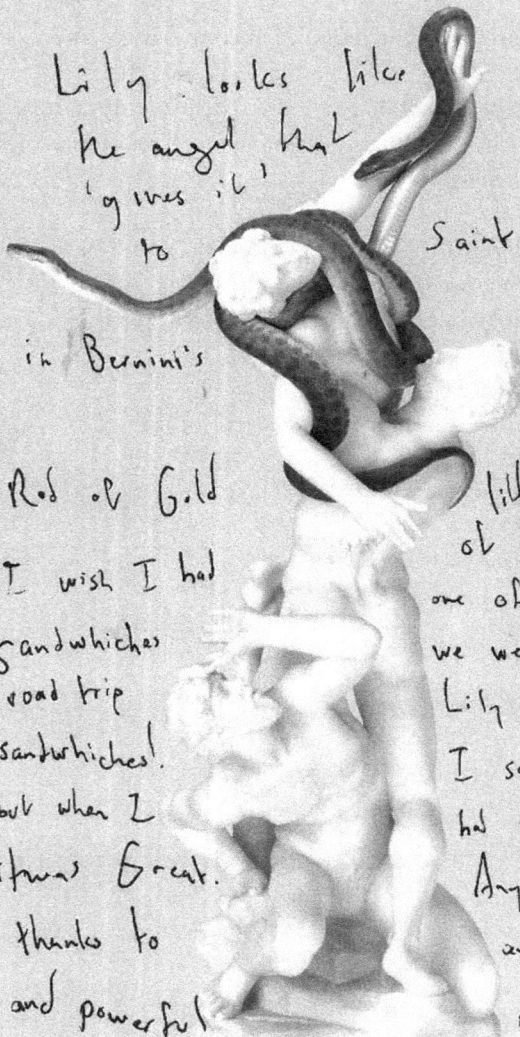

Hellover Pikey Fitness Regime

A Hellover Pikey Fitness Regime is ours to keeps
Running Snifting Combining Drifting
   Chroming Trifling Boxing
'Rattle yr Dags, Percy!'
My liver at least is alive to the mystery of it

W'its patterns of fossilized lightning
Preferring an infinite capsize
 A sort of curious spasming goes on and on
    Let's leave
immediately.

Blotter Betty was a savage kisser
1800-D-e-s-i r -e   'I don't wanna
                    I don't think so . . .
Cunties in perpetuity!
He used to have a lot of the Dareness
             Still dressed by 's mother though
Pwrd by Rage, yes, but whatre we burning up?
Only yr. Angelic Chubb my persistent
                    counterfeiter

Praise
        Winona
     Saint Winona Ryder   patroness of the right kinds of
    summery friction
Shoplifting Masturbating   polishing the knack
The Debacler wind in the curlicues   helps make these withering
        golden c_rds
            obsearve

The transition of the feast of the assumption to its fecal condition
(can I get tight pants in here?)

That's not a brawl that's a fugal dialogue

If only we were more feeble and obedient (we are we are)
replenish your smooth-bore arterials with acres of canker-green
as when in the bosky dell of the gut
                    narcotics bloom

    headed for the Ballyferknackery
        via the ballyvoguery

m.guts are ever in thr favourite place
m. billiards are all after falling out
 what saith the pig lobby?
Somewhere in the valley gropes the Daemon
 Sorting the population fingerly as his own
                            Cantaloupe

There's nothing in the news not even a discovered head
                of bog butter.

Dear Josephine I am compelled
 To loiter here a lttle longer where they are all s.mad and hungry
    Yr. friend & booseyboy
            'Nibbles' Bonaparte

The ship we desireth is made badly by hand
   The wrecks of the Belfast the Ballina and the Ballinphunta it's hard
      to know
w/ whom to go down to go down

The spirit hounds are loose on the gloaming   too fast for the wind
    who would make love to them
 & anyway they are a lot of coves
hundsfottisch
    hundsfettisch
       hundsfottery
To speak doggerel so naughtily and saucily

 Helping the girl with one arm move house
T' other arm lost to child polio
We work filling the truck . . . she walks
Here she comes back from the shops at Bellambi
Held in her prosthetic claw (porcelain covered in T'ang Dynasty cranes)
    A mystery bag
 'I got us a dead chicken to eat' >>
                        Stania.

I mean you can't have giant cement vulvas appearing everplace for
    public worship
It's too much   too much like the Sheila na gig
 Had to be secreted in the co'ner this knowledge is not for everybody

cleave instead to the farmers wire to tittilate the heart with forty volts to
    tittilate the heart
                                        in pursuit of eggs for yr bacon
                                                or a daffodil
all this commentated completely by the tattler sportscaster
                            Dougal Beatty
Dooby Dee a Rub-a-Dub
these teeth the expensive ruins of Babylon

the slang for being a sucker changed from day to day didntit
 the thyroid glands all cling to their party bags brimming with
    black parcels
                            of old blood
                                *
I took ma snakeskin on a roadtrip past Coolangatta I hope you don't'
    mind.
Th whole fuckin street is smells of splurge laurel/
But . . . . . . I love primitive formless anarchy.

Me old pagan motherbells bye
        bye Sharyn
I finally buried my horde back in Faerye Meadow
Immaculate w/ a predator's sense of careful
            expenditure

That we loved to get high is true.
    The vissicitudes   . . .   (double punctum) (ouch)
 Olivia o'Donnell!   I'm writing you

(why shouldn't I) to tell you of the East Coast Fancier's Club
Whose razo d'amour is for   West Coast Spunkies
     Gifted in the nuisancical
My sweet scalp-smelling livery
Olivia emerges at the head of the garden party
   A heavy Voluptuous sprite

What we have here is the perfect likeness of the Perth Sharpies Perpetual
     Sailing Trophy!
Feral Prima
                              Donna
O won't you be my Handsome Joe Byrne and I'll be your perpetually
     deceptive
                                        Aaron Sherritt

          After three days on the lacey
     I've got the bon bon irrits
          Ripe for Pricking
                    *

                    I must establish m.own mobile purloinery

                         *

Bone under the sign of Saturn I'll take my tartan with the suicidal
     Lairds of Gight
          Rough with the Rose's head
          In m. pocket
The world is so full of coincidences and coinfluences
A'rovin and A'ravin down the side of every hill the same
                              *

                    *

God its lovely on the Ballybogey Road County Cork; I just went on
a 'google maps' holiday there

The friend I met in no time at all:

Lets's become highwaypersons . . . I will be the gorgeous acolyte of
Cptn. Moonlite

& you can be the Babeh Snakeh
Feared by roadworkers from Avenal to Gundagai

Capitalism!

Like teen kissing Like bourgeois clover
Like freckles on m.tits
    You have the courage to continue thank god

I knew you would

The Brogo Rotolactor continues to rotolactate
  Centripetally spraying drops of milk
   On our fev'rish cheeks
   Defying even 'the thrill of acquisition'

Famous scenes at Peechelba
Famous scenes at Pflahert's Hotel

We recovered your booty from the park again, filthy as it was with
    quarks and charms
Dandy Hams Dandy Hams, I want to be your dandy hams

                     Balls nasty
              Sweet balls ecstasy and a little tumble in the shower

Started hissing most often times like an adolescing snakeh   the
    vissicitudes
  double puncture marks wherein went the sauce for . . .
Black poesy

& I'm more than a little in love with my sister
                           Im going to clean my Little
                           Cowboy Tears
                       with my little
                       cowboy rag

Do you think we are too rough to join the Overjoyed Company of the
    seven troubadours of Toulouse?

' *Abso-bloomin-lutely*' shae cried
                a rare spasm of some deliberate plebian slang
                    Like trefoil island it's there seething especially when it isn't
                        Sex sausages a deadly swim and whiskey with
    Bucky Maynard
                    For which there is no brochure

Theres some lichenated moss and clover growing there on your shoulder
I guess this means we're getting less speedie
Though you still come home after the party stamping the ground like
    a steroidal
 Half-satyr, Half cottage-pie
Pick your nose like the maestro

Peace &
    Dedeucedness

  where's my Bucephalus my Pegasus my Berruary Dick? Sose I can
    ply my bruising trade
You've been brushed by the raven   dress like the raven even
  In yr. shit-laden cackledaks   (caca-dells)

Rippishly inspissated   bon-ton jackdaw

Plug reading is a pretty dark art I shall not

Trust the lady or the man who will not kiss their plugs
at the moment of replacing them

'you smell like yve been on it for days, Tinkerbell!'
'I have, Miladdy   ginger wine potatoes porkspray & Byronic
                                                soda
Forever rolling over at the Weasel-Head Hotel

May this poem continue as hematopoiesis   nourished in turn by its
        own bloodbursts
    Lymphoblast becoming natural killer cells (we hope)
Gibed (gybed) by Sheral (Cheryl) about my much admired
    Les dents du Bonheur (th mitherficken teeth of bliss!)
As natural as Queen Elizabeth Regina II in a bondage collar
Or Goldie cruising past your window in a shopping trolly

Flirt-deserving I go to town
now, not so much tender as bacon-footed if you come
                    To know what I mean

Caught in the ancient crossfire that's the racket
        Of the Gods
    It's a vendetta

Sometimes the sounds of flies just cruising the room is so

                                                  Mortadella.

This is Dougald Beatty calling
       From the bowels of the soft-serve machine I think me
Of Annie, freckled exchequer of the pubic baths of Fitzrovia
Of Bonnie, lately made a Leprachaun's bride
Of Tzortzolopino, the Greatest Queen Who ever pulled pranks
Of Lona and Carc who retired to the Dyke Pantisocracy
                                       Of Old Jindabyne

Hello Steeplechasers

The silver heirlooms are now in the air itself   are the air itself
 God the future is so sexy.
Some Sufi told me god sent Satan away so he would have someone to
    have a crush on.
Like Permanently.
                                        So Bitcheh!

Acknowledgements

Poems from *The Jewelled Shillelagh* first appeared in *Australian Book Review*, *Cordite Poetry Review*, *Rabbit* and *Redroom Poetry*.